Cult of Two

Cult of Two

Michael Faudet

Andrews McMeel
PUBLISHING®

For Lang,

In your eyes I see myself. I see the love
we never thought was possible.

Cult of Two

INTRODUCTION

Cult of Two is my fifth book, but it feels a lot like my first.

For those of you who are familiar with my work, don't be surprised if you discover the ghost of *Dirty Pretty Things* hiding somewhere within the pages.

In fact, I should warn you now—*this book is fucking haunted*.

Things may go bump in the night when you read it.

The words are dripping with magic and mischief. So please be careful not to let this rather strange book possess you. Like it did me, writing it.

Red roses and broken hearts.

My gift to you.

On this cold winter's night.

All my love,

— Michael xo

I Am the Girl

In the quiet times—
    when I think about my life,
    you come to me,
    banging pots and pans
    inside my head,
    your voice screaming—
    I am the girl
    you'll never forget.

A CERTAIN SOMETHING

You had a certain something about you. A strange, brooding darkness that was incredibly sexy and somewhat impossible to ignore. Whenever you smiled, it was like the sun breaking through the storm.

THE LAST DAYS OF SUMMER

Perhaps it was the rhythmic chant of cicadas that lulled me into this calm state of being. The last days of summer—in all its glorious sunsets and fading colors. Nature's delightful, intoxicating, narcotic. Freeing my mind from the chaos of simply breathing.

A MIDNIGHT CALL

Be careful—
someone might be listening.

I can almost hear
    that rebellious smile
    in your silent reply.

The one you wear
    so well on rosy lips.

Your hushed moans
    begin again,
    becoming louder.

Pretty mouth—
    pressed up against
    the hotel phone.

LOVE DEFINED

Burn all the dictionaries, tear up the tired metaphors, and tell the poets to go to hell. For you are the true definition of love. The only one I shall ever need.

Only You Could Write

A wave explodes—
    the slow rumble
    of thunder,
    swirling sand
    and seaweed.

A paperback novel—
    resting on a bed
    of broken seashells,
    the pages open—
    a sentence underlined
    in pencil gray.

You kiss me—
    the scent of weed
    lingering on lips,
    only you could
    write a sunset
    this beautiful.

Holding hands
    beneath tangerine skies,
    a sea of rolling fire
    and flying fish,
    a daydream made real—
    in the shutter click
    of an eyelid.

Sticky Tape

My fingers pull
 clear sticky tape
 from nipples,
 just as you orgasm—
 how exquisite
 the pleasure found,
 in so little pain.

OUR FIRST BREATH

When we enter this world,
    knowing nothing of life,
    how ironic—
    our first breath
    begins with tears.

HOW STRANGE

How strange these late nights—dreaming of sleep. Listening to the owls sing and thinking about you.

DAFFODILS

My obsession for you—
    black ribbons untied
    in a cheap airport motel.

The scent of sex
    still clinging to your legs.

Eyes mesmerized,
    spellbound—
    searching for answers.

Do daffodils cry
    when the sun is shining?

IT'S THE LITTLE THINGS

It's the little things I love the most. The beauty found in the
mundane. Strawberry jam and toast crumbs—a morning kiss.

CHOPPING ONIONS

Chopping onions
    on a Wednesday night—
    how strange the things
    we remember,
    when our world
    is falling apart,
    disintegrating—
    in slow motion.

I'm not sure
    who cried the most,
    impossible to tell
    when tears hide
    behind tears.

Not that it matters,
    when a bottle
    is empty,
    the wine finished—
    and so are we.

YOU AND ME

You once told me that the shortest distance between two points is a straight line. Unfortunately the same can't be said for finding love.

I HAD NO IDEA

A light rain shower
    in bright sunshine—
    that's how you
    hid your sadness,
    my eyes blinded
    by your smile,
    mistaking the tears
    for happiness.

A Secret Place

I can take you to a secret place, somewhere not far from here,
where the desert stars sing lullabies to the brokenhearted.

AFTER THE PARTY

A sweet hint
    of summer strawberries,
    on glistening lips
    stained sticky red.

Our first kiss—
    under a waning moon,
    adrift in a sea
    of silent black.

A bra strap falls,
    breathy notes
    by fingers played—
    on blades of green
    beneath twisted trees.

A whisper of silk
    on midnight thigh,
    as panties drop
    with gentle sigh.

NEVER US

It was always about you. Seldom me. And never us.

You Moved On

You moved on—
    before the dust could settle.

So fast—
    not even a single strand
    of silver cobweb
    was left behind
    to hold on to.

No spider could spin
    a web that quickly.

ALL THE TIME I POSSESS

All the time I possess, from milliseconds to hours, blessed days to precious years—I give it all to you.

TO BE IN LOVE

Dappled sunlight
   slowly dancing
   on goose-bumped
   winter skin.

A dawn begins
   for naked bodies,
   a mad dash—
   from silver sand
   to waiting sea.

How glorious it is
   to be in love,
   to be young—
   to be free.

IN LOVE WITH WORDS

I'm not just in love with words, I'm possessed by them. My life consumed by the twenty-six letters of the alphabet and all the countless possibilities they bring to a page. How beautiful this world of dust and cobwebs. Where the pen is mightier than the vacuum cleaner.

FINGERS BURNT

A bad relationship can be defined by the striking of a match. The longer you hold on to it, the greater the likelihood of getting your fingers burnt.

LOOK AT ME

"Look at me," you cry—
    a hand between
    your legs.

Hardcore masturbation
    in all its primal glory.

A hips rising,
    eyes closing,
    mouth opening,
    toes curling—
    private show
    for one.

HERDING CATS

You told me to stop letting my emotions run away from me. But how can I? Herding cats in the dark with one arm tied behind my back would be easier than controlling these feelings I have for you.

BURNT TOAST

A wisp of smoke
    in morning sun,
    a slice of toast,
    ignored, forgotten.

Left to burn—
    its meaning lost,
    the slow decay
    of happiness,
    from golden brown
    to cinder black.

Not even honey
    can take away
    the bitter aftertaste.

When depression
    is served up,
    in bite-sized pieces.

A Slow Pirouette

You took my hand and made it yours. Guiding my fingers beneath the hem of your panties. Showing me exactly how you wanted to be touched—like a ballerina in the spotlight doing a slow pirouette.

CRAZY

It was the fear
   of losing you,
   that drove me away—
   I realize now
   just how crazy
   that sounds.

It was my insecurity,
   my self-doubt,
   that slowly trapped me—
   like a straightjacket
   tailor-made for one.

And not even
   your undying love
   could free me—
   from myself.

NEVER CLOSE ENOUGH

There's no denying we had chemistry and a strong desire to be together. Yet somehow you were never willing to make a commitment. Close but never close enough.

Like walking on a tightrope in high heels.

WE DIDN'T FALL IN LOVE

We didn't fall in love—
    it was more like
    the slow descent
    of a feather
    on a windless day.

A leaky tap
    filling an ocean,
    drip by drip.

Like our world
    had forgotten
    how to turn.

In a universe
    high on morphine.

HAPPY NEW YEAR

Years may come and go but my love for you is a never-ending fireworks show.

PERHAPS

The inability to be decisive—
    to ponder love
    with no conclusion,
    to give hope
    when all is hopeless,
    there is no divide
    more divisive.

Never Again

You asked me to give you a second chance and all you gave me back was a repeated mistake.

UNFORGETTABLE

I can still
       remember when—
       we carved our love
       into the bark
       of winter trees.

Your smile
       never forgotten—
       always found.

Wandering—
       in the forest
       of past lovers.

BLACK RAIN

The pitter-patter
of droplets bleak,
no end in sight,
no grief complete—
this endless sorrow
of which I speak.

HOW LOVE FEELS

A lull in the storm. The sparkle of sunshine held by the rain. This is how love feels. Just when you thought everything was lost.

SCREAMING SEX

Swirling smoke
   from the last drag
   on a dying joint.

You strike a pose
   wearing black leather
   crotchless panties.

Giving me—*that look*.

Doe-eyed innocence
   meets bitten lip.

Beautifully perverse,
   breathtaking—
   a silent surrender.

Screaming sex
   without saying
   a single word.

Rebellious Spirit

Love is a rebellious spirit that doesn't seek permission or ask for approval.

UNBREAKABLE

Thrown sticks
and hurled stones,
all the fucking lies
and dirty tricks—
never let them
break you.

INSIDE EVERY CHERRY

In matters of love it's tempting to be picky. But never forget, inside every cherry, *no matter how delicious*—you'll always find a stone.

THE ELEVENTH FIRST DATE

"I do rather enjoy these random little drives into the country. How we always seem to find a quiet place to park. Far away from prying eyes," Sophia said, quickly checking her lipstick in the rearview mirror.

"This spot looks perfect," I replied.

Sophia pressed down on the brake pedal and slowly steered the white Bentley into the rest stop, which was surrounded by beautiful oak trees and overlooked a vista of rolling green fields.

"Yes this will do nicely," she said, turning off the ignition.

I could already hear the excitement in her voice as she unclipped her seat belt and pulled up her gray pleated cotton skirt, revealing a pair of white panties and pale winter thighs.

"You know, this dirty little game of yours is quite mad and terribly kinky."

"Oh, hush now," she cooed, opening her legs a fraction wider on the tan leather seat. "Just pretend it's our first date again and give my pussy a damn good fingering."

—

The afternoon sun slowly slipped away behind the trees—leaving behind a dying sky of sunset orange and shadowy clouds.

"It's such a crying shame we only get to live a single lifetime," Sophia sighed.

I took her delicate hand in mine and pressed it to my lips. Softly kissing each finger. "Every second spent with you is a lifetime. Every hour—an eternity."

I WANT YOUR LOVE

I want your love—
      every color
      of the rainbow.

Every drop
      of winter rain.

And when you
      give it to me—
      it will never
      be enough.

PERFECTION

Perfection is a race that can never be won.

RIDING THE SUBWAY

Lifeless verse—
     written with a dead pen.

Black ink spilt
     on a cold December,
     riding the subway
     in an endless loop.

Where lonely drunks
     meet rejected lovers.

A swig of sorrow
     inside every bottle,
     but never enough
     to dull the pain.

A brown paper bag
     therapy session—
     of shattered dreams
     and broken hearts.

PRIORITIES

Possessions are temporary. There are no storage units in the afterlife.

THE MAD PRINCESS

She wore a silver tiara
and white bikini,
dancing backward
across the sand.

In her palace—
only madness reigns.

This princess
doing somersaults,
chasing thunderbolts—
drinking champagne
in the rain.

THE HARDEST GOODBYE

I knew I had to set you free. To put my feelings aside and let love slip through my fingers. It wasn't easy. But if you try to keep hold of a butterfly—you run the risk of crushing it.

THE BROOM CLOSET

There was an almost surreal element to Serena's sexual desires.

And tonight was no exception.

There were no scattered rose petals or tiny lit candles.

Just a trail of strawberry sherbet sprinkled down the hallway. Which I followed until I reached the end point—a broom closet. Where a pink postage note was stuck to the door with the words, *Sex lives here,* scribbled in green pen.

I took a deep breath and opened the door.

Serena was standing inside. Her naked body lit by a single lightbulb. I could see she had tipped the last remains of the sherbet over her pussy.

She flashed me a mischievous smile and said, "Lick it clean."

Her words were not so much a request but a command. So I did as I was told. I knelt down on the wooden floorboards and roughly parted her pussy lips with my fingers. I began to lick and suck on her clitoris, feeling the tingle of the sherbet on my tongue.

Serena pressed her hips into my face and started to moan.

I kept up the rhythm, slow and steady, until I felt her hand tap my shoulder. It was the signal to stop and give her what she so desperately desired.

A good hard fucking.

Now it was my turn to be the boss.

I got up off my knees, stood up, and unbuckled my black leather belt. Threading it through the loops, one by one, until it was free.

Then I gently wrapped the belt around Serena's neck. Slowly tightening the loop so that the buckle pressed down on her throat.

"Are you ready for your present?"

"Yes," she replied, looking directly into my eyes.

I unzipped my fly and gave the belt a firm pull.

Serena gasped.

"I fucking love it!" she cried—her cheeks flushing red.

I forced my hard cock deep inside her tight pussy.

Serena bit down on her lip and began to moan loudly.

This just made me want to fuck her even harder. So I lifted Serena up into my arms and felt her legs grip my waist. Pressing her back hard against the wall, I started to slam my cock in and out of her wet pussy.

Sending us both into a sex-crazed frenzy.

Her tits slapping against my chest with every thrust of my cock.

The pleasure intense and uncontrollable.

I watched her pretty mouth slowly open.

The orgasm exploding between her legs.

—

We stood in the hallway.

Catching our breath.

Cum dripping down the inside of Serena's thigh.

I removed the belt from her neck. Tracing the pink line left behind on her pale skin with my finger.

She placed her hands on my shoulders and stared into my eyes. "Do you know what you do to me? How you make me feel?"

"Glad that you married me?" I replied smiling.

Serena laughed. Pulling me closer and pressing her warm lips to my ear.

"Happy anniversary," she whispered.

CHANGE THE WORLD

Poetry can change your life, but don't expect it to change the world. Only you have the power to take on that challenge. A poem can stir the heart, but it can't cast a vote.

When Will I See You Again?

So many promises
    wrapped up in excuses,
    always tomorrow
    but never today.

TURN ME ON

Not a word is said. You turn me on with just your eyes.
Fingers gripping my hard cock. My pleasure held in the palm
of your hand.

RAGE AGAINST LOVE

Spare me your pity—
    the worthless platitudes,
    just let me rage
    against love.

Set my heart free—
    just leave me be,
    to rip the stars
    from the night sky,
    while I scream—
    go fuck yourself
    to the moon.

Please—
    pretty please,
    just let me rage
    against love.

THE TWO OF US

How easy the glass
    slipped from our hands,
    shattered shards—
    the jagged truth
    crystal clear,
    left to sparkle
    in the dullness.

All our energy
    put into breaking—
    what was already broken.

RISK EVERYTHING

How precarious the fine line between acceptance and rejection. Yet, here I am again—placing another bet on the table. Going all in. Willing to risk everything for a chance to win this stupid game we call love.

Awake

I became so obsessed with you, that I even convinced myself that you loved me.

GUILTY SEX

Temptation comes—
  a stage is set,
  your lifted skirt
  with panties wet,
  the sweet allure
  of guilty sex,
  you giving head,
  lips cherry red—
  fucking in your
  parents' bed.

SUNSHINE IN RAINDROPS

I could speak of your generosity of spirit—the sublime language spoken by your heart. But it is your laughter I miss the most. The rarest gift you ever gave me.

IT WAS THE NIGHT

It was the night—
    when stars fell
    from your lips.

My hands
    on your hips,
    pulling you closer.

Our parting wish—
    to be forever,
    held together
    in a kiss.

THE EXPLICIT REQUEST

You pushed me hard against the tree and slid your hand down the inside of my jeans.

"I know you respect me and that's lovely," you said kissing my lips. "However tonight, please spare me your polite words and gentle hands."

I felt your slender fingers grasp my cock as you whispered into my ear.

"I don't want you to fuck my pretty pussy—*I want you to destroy it.*"

HUMILITY

Humility is the ability to celebrate a victory and not let your success defeat you.

REJECTION

"Would you like to smoke this joint with me?"

Sophia had a habit of asking rhetorical questions. A well-practiced distraction technique she had perfected over the years, and one I couldn't possibly resist. No matter how hard I tried.

"I really do need to get this book written," I replied, hunched over my laptop at the kitchen table, trying my best to ignore her piercing gaze pointed in my direction. "I'm already two weeks past the publisher's deadline, and my first manuscript was rejected."

"Rejected? You never told me that," Sophia said, twirling a lock of red hair with her fingers.

"It's not the kind of news you go shouting from the rooftops. But it's okay."

Sophia sat down next to me and fired up the joint. Blowing a cloud of swirling smoke into the air. "I'd be beside myself if that happened to me. I have a real issue with rejection."

"It used to bother me a lot too. Especially in terms of creativity. You pour your heart and soul into a project, spending countless days and nights perfecting it, only to have it dismissed on a whim."

"Well, you seem remarkably calm about it all," Sophia said smiling.

"Rejection is a learning curve and it took me a while to come to terms with it. Until I realized it was just a temporary setback and an opportunity to do something even better. Now when it happens to me, I think of myself as a tiny rubber ball. *The harder I get hit—the faster I bounce back.*"

"I love that! Honestly, you should be a philosopher not a poet," she exclaimed enthusiastically, passing me the glowing joint.

I took a long hard drag and instantly felt the effects. "Fuck, this is strong stuff!"

Sophia burst out laughing. "Hey, I just thought of a title for your next book."

"Really? What is it?" I asked.

"*Self-Help for Stoners.*"

LET IT GO

Never let anger get the better of you. No matter how justified it might seem at the time, in hindsight, it seldom solves or changes anything for the better. Find the courage to forgive yourself, even if you can't forgive them.

IN YOUR SILENCE

In your silence—it is the essence of who you are, the kindness that defines your heart, that speaks to me the loudest.

DEVOTION

Every Sunday—
    a sermon served,
    in silk robes
    and silver rings.

The gold plate
    passed around—
    collecting coins
    from empty pockets.

Come Monday—
    we work for
    our daily bread.

Bought with sweat
    and broken backs.

Praying—
    for a miracle.

FAR TOO LATE

The inexplicable,
    in hindsight—
    explained.

The opened gate
    I tried to close—
    far too late.

Can you hear
    the echo of regret?

Bouncing
    off the walls
    of a heart—
    broken.

WRITTEN BY YOU

When I read the words you wrote, what really hurt me the most, was that they were written by you.

SECOND HELPING

It was past 3 a.m. when Todd stumbled through the front door of the apartment and staggered into the bedroom. The familiar naughty boy grin plastered across his face as he rocked back and forth at the end of the bed. The stench of cheap liquor and stale cigarettes on his breath.

Sarah was sitting up in the bed, dressed in her favorite pink flannel dressing gown. She put down the cookbook she was reading and stared at Todd's bloodshot eyes.

"I'm sorry, babe. Got caught up with the boys again and lost track of time," he slurred.

"That's okay. How about you get undressed and into bed. You must be exhausted," Sarah said softly.

Todd flashed a crooked smirk as he collapsed onto the bed next to her like a sack of old rags. His head hitting the pillow. Eyes closing shut as he passed out.

Sarah hopped out of bed and took off his muddy shoes. She gently folded her half of the white comforter over him and left the bedroom, switching off the light on her way out.

It wasn't the first time Sarah had been forced to sleep on the sofa. She pulled a blanket over her body, rested her head on a cushion, and stared up at the ceiling, listening in the dark to Todd's thunderous snoring coming from the bedroom.

It was late in the morning and the sun was streaming through the kitchen window.

Sarah checked her watch and wandered over to the oven.

Peering through the glass door she could see the golden crust of the pie and knew it was ready. She reached for the oven gloves from the counter and put them on.

When the pie came out of the oven, Sarah eyed it with a satisfied smile. It was perfectly cooked and filled the entire ceramic baking dish. She placed it down on the stove top and reached up for a white dinner plate from the shelf.

"Ooh, my fucking head!"

Sarah heard Todd's chesty moan coming from the bedroom, followed by a loud, rumbling fart. He was finally awake.

She neatly cut a generous slice of the pie and placed it on the plate with a spatula. She carried it quickly into the bedroom with a small bottle of water she had taken from the fridge.

Todd was still in his disheveled suit, greasy hair flopped over his forehead, trying to summon up the strength to crawl out of bed.

"I thought you might want breakfast in bed, sweetheart," Sarah said, placing the plate down in front of him.

Todd reached over and snatched the bottle of water from her hand.

He unscrewed the cap and poured the water into his throat, gulping it down and throwing the empty bottle onto the carpet. He looked at the slice of pie sitting on the plate.

"Smells bloody marvelous," he exclaimed, grinning.

"Let me go get you a knife and fork," Sarah replied.

"Nah, fuck that. I'll use my hands."

Sarah watched Todd tear the pie apart with his chubby fingers, shoving large mouthfuls of pastry into his mouth—the thick brown gravy running down the stubble on his chin.

"What is it? Beef? Tastes a bit like chicken too."

"Oh, it's just a little something I whipped up. A new recipe," Sarah said. "I hope you like it."

Todd burped and wiped his sticky fingers on the comforter. "Like it? I fucking love it! Be a good girl and go get me another slice."

Sarah dutifully picked up the dirty plate off the bed and returned to the kitchen, where she cut another large slice of the pie before walking back into the bedroom.

"There you go, sweetheart. Enjoy!"

She handed Todd the plate and watched him start to devour the second helping of pie. He smacked his lips as he swallowed large chunks of gristle and soggy meat.

Sarah left him to finish eating his breakfast.

When she got back to the kitchen, she looked down at her gold wedding ring. She let out a little sigh and slid it off her finger. Throwing it into the trash can.

The ring rattled against the sides of the empty cans of cheap dog food sitting inside.

Sarah couldn't hold back the smile any longer and chuckled to herself.

A wave of euphoria swept through her body as she skipped across the living room to the front door where her packed suitcase lay waiting.

She picked up it up and quietly slipped out of the apartment.

IF SOMEONE REALLY CARES

If someone really cares about you, they will do everything they possibly can to right the wrong.

Those who secretly can't be bothered—just make excuses.

STRANGERS IN THE SNOW

When the snow came—
   I thought of you.

The magical night
   we spent together.

Kissing in parkas—
   melting snowflakes
   with rosy lips.

Making promises—
   we couldn't
   possibly keep.

PLEASURE BOUND

Ropes tied—
    her tethered wrists.

Vibrator pressed
    on swollen clit.

Pleasure bound
    with writhing hips.

My fingers fucking
    pretty lips.

Her silent scream—
    the whipped cream,
    with a cherry
    on top.

A NEW ROMANCE

Will you be
    my new romance?

A first sentence
    of a love story.

The beginning
    of my everything.

UNDER THE PIER

You kiss me with lips that taste of sex and pink bubble gum.

Standing in the shadows. Our bare feet buried in the wet sand—the warm summer sea swirling around our ankles.

The teddy bear I won for you at the fair, carried quietly away by the outgoing tide.

Our innocence lost beneath a rotting wood and barnacle sky.

Under the pier.

WHEN THE ROMANCE GOES

I remember a time when you made me daisy chains.
Now you just mow the lawn.

TRASH TALK

How amusing
   it must be,
   to sip poison
   with your friends,
   to crack jokes
   at my expense—
   to laugh behind
   my back.

Never knowing
   it's actually me,
   who is laughing
   the hardest.

Thrilled to bits,
   deliriously ecstatic—
   over the fucking moon!

To finally see
   the back of you.

THE PAST

The past is the past. You can't change it. But you can cherish it, celebrate it, laugh about it, learn from it, and take the happy memories with you. What really matters is today. The new page that's waiting to be written. Knowing you have your whole life ahead of you and the best is yet to come.

RED COTTON PANTIES

You love to touch yourself with your panties on. Lying in the bed next to me. Your hand under the hem, fingers softly rubbing your clitoris.

A dark wet patch spreading across the cheap red cotton.

I place my hand over yours. So I can feel the movement—the rhythmic circles becoming faster, as you pleasure yourself with eyes closed.

My lips press against your ear and whisper dirty pretty things.

"Does your pussy feel good?"

"Spread your legs a little wider."

"Imagine having a big cock stretching you open—fucking you."

The breathy moans become louder.

Quicker.

When the orgasm finally comes, I pull on your pink nipples with my fingers. Making your hips buck uncontrollably. Legs writhing with every intense wave.

—

A beautiful moment of dreamy calm.

Your pretty face flushed and a quiet smile resting on your lips. I watch as you slide your legs out of the soaking wet panties and reach down for them.

You gaze deeply into my eyes and speak ever so softly.

"How would you like to feel my dirty panties on your hard cock?"

You don't wait for a reply. My eyes close as you wrap them around the shaft of my cock. I feel the damp fabric and your sticky juice on my skin.

Your hand pulls my thick cock up and down.

Harder.

Faster.

Until you feel the familiar throb beneath your delicate fingers. Biting down on your lip while you watch me cum all over your panties.

Hearing me say your name.

Over and over again.

SIX SECONDS

This can't be true.

Reading a text—
    doubting my doubts,
    drinking vinegar
    laced with disaster.

I've met someone.

Six years destroyed—
    in six seconds.

MASS DELUSION

Melting ice caps
    and burning trees,
    dolphins strangled
    in plastic seas,
    temperatures rising
    by alarming degrees,
    poisoned rivers
    and dying bees,
    a crying world
    brought to its knees.

But don't panic—
    Instagram's back up.

A DIFFERENT PERSON

It took me a while to realize you had changed. No longer the same person I fell in love with all those years ago. Funny how I used to miss you when we were apart. Now I always miss you whenever we're together.

UNKNOWN PLEASURES

Pearly suns—
    buttons undone,
    one by one,
    in a garden
    of wild orchids.

On bended knees—
    your fingertips,
    with open lips,
    give ecstasy
    a name.

IN YOUR EYES

In your eyes I see myself. I see the love we never thought was possible.

TIME HEALS ALL

There comes a time
   when the crying stops,
   no more tissues left
   in the empty box.

The chains unchained—
   the locks unlocked.

A heart slowly mends—
   tick tock, tick tock.

The hours passing
   on the kitchen clock.

Fearless Girl

Her power comes
    from deep within,
    inside a heart
    her bravery sings,
    a self-belief—
    her smile brings,
    this fearless girl
    with angel wings.

A LITTLE PART OF ME

When you left—you took a little part of me. Not that I will be needing it back anytime soon. For what use is a smile to me now?

DISPOSABLE

I was just a summer fling,
    a pretty plaything,
    to parade in front
    of your friends.

Clinging to your arm,
    while yours
    carved a new notch
    on the fucking
    bedpost.

OVERWHELMED

Surely it's irresponsible to love someone this much. If so—
then I'm the happiest fool alive.

OLD NEWS

Last night—
    my innocent face,
    made the front page
    of your heart.

The girl of your dreams—
    the headline read.

When morning came,
    how quickly
    the story changed.

I became—
    just another name,
    in a long line
    of lovers—
    thrown away.

Like yesterday's
    newspaper.

Rise Above It

We can wallow in the mire or we can rise above it. Yes, it can be a struggle to pull ourselves out of the oozing mud of negativity and pettiness. But when we do, it's remarkable how liberating it feels to be back in control of our lives. To be able to redirect all that wasted energy into something that showcases the very best in us. And is infinitely more worthwhile, more rewarding, and far more creative.

My Fear

To fall in love—
     is what I feared
     the most.

To have my heart
     dragged—
     from pillar to post.

To discover
     a certainty,
     was just—
     an *almost*.

THE TRUTH

The truth is fast becoming an endangered species. It's up to all of us to protect it.

MOUSETRAPS

My head—
    a dusty attic,
    filled with faded
    love letters,
    and forgotten
    mousetraps.

Yet here I am,
    thinking of you again—
    eyes closed,
    walking barefoot,
    reliving the pain
    with every step.

OUR PRETEND SUMMER

You always loved to play make-believe on rainy afternoons.

Blue cellophane sticky-taped to a bedroom window. Sipping strawberry daiquiris in chipped coffee cups. Basking in the warm glow of a plastic fan heater.

Dreaming of Saint-Tropez beaches and listening to Lana Del Rey. Two misfits in mismatched pajamas. Peeling oranges and fucking with the lights on.

DISAPPOINTMENT

Just when I thought my life was going in the right direction—
disappointment was waiting around the corner.

I OFTEN WISH

As years pass,
    I often wish
    I could outrun
    time itself—
    to slip away,
    if only for a day,
    to spend another
    twenty-four hours
    with you.

HORIZON

When I look to the horizon, I never see it as the end of my world. More the beginning. Where a new adventure is waiting to be discovered.

THE STAIRCASE

When it comes to finding true love, some people just get lucky. The elevator doors magically open and they get an easy ride to the top. The rest of us have to take the fucking staircase. One miserable step at a time.

Our Little Garden

Like a wild rose—
 her petals free,
 to greet the sun
 inside of me.

For what is true
 is mine to give,
 in this place
 we call love—
 our little garden
 of happiness.

HEAVEN

A feather-soft touch,
  the lips of an angel
  descending on mine—
  heaven in a kiss.

Love's Light

Only love—
    can burn this bright,
    the brilliance
    of its light,
    like a million
    moonlit nights,
    in your eyes
    it shines—
    tonight.

STAIN ON MY HEART

My angry words spilt—like red wine tipped from a glass by my own hand. I only have myself to blame for this stain on my heart.

BLACK UMBRELLAS

So many beautiful
    speeches made,
    the life you lived—
    revered with tears.

Silent sentences—
    spoken in the rain.

Such a shame,
    our best words
    come last.

Always said—
    when it's too late.

KALEIDOSCOPE

Dropping acid
   in the bathtub.

Laughing at dragons
   swinging from
   the chandelier.

Incense burning—
   our names written
   in curling smoke
   and sandalwood.

Purple stars
   running from
   rainbow taps.

Kissing lips—
   that sing
   of summer.

The sweet taste
   of marmalade—
   cantaloupes,
   and cotton candy.

TO LIVE A LIE

How beautiful—
    to live a lie.

To imagine—
    you and me
    together.

To catch a glimpse
    of a shooting star.

Piercing the darkness
    of my loneliness.

TOMORROW NEVER KNOWS

We loved each other so much that it was unthinkable we would ever tear ourselves apart.

But somehow we did. Neither one of us able to pinpoint exactly why or how the impossible happened. And when we searched our hearts for answers, we only found more questions.

The only logical solution we could both agree on, was to go our separate ways.

As the months passed, it became clear that any thought of remaining even friends was never going to happen. The "how are you?" phone calls stopped, the random texts fizzled out, and all contact was eventually lost.

And then out of the blue, one warm July morning, our paths crossed again. You stepped out of a cab just as I was buying a hotdog from a street vendor. Our eyes met, and the smiles quickly followed. We gave each other a hug and you suggested I ditch the hotdog and we go grab a coffee instead.

While I sat across the table watching you sip your cappuccino, I realized something was different about you. The way that you looked at me. How the very words you spoke took on that old familiar tone I thought had vanished forever.

Something had changed inside of me too.

I felt the tingles of joy and excitement returning, shooting through my body, igniting my heart like a schoolboy on his first date. And then I realized what it was. *My God, I was falling in love.*

And so were you.

—

We fell out of love just so we could fall back in.

SAINT-GERMAIN

God is in the details
    you always said.

A blue angel
    dancing on my
    shot glass.

Knocking back
    a flaming Sambuca
    at 7:07 a.m.

Sprinkling caviar
    on poached eggs—
    tiny black pearls
    of salty heaven.

A Calum Hood
    bass riff—
    on my headphones.

Writing poetry
    in a hotel room
    in Paris.

Paradise—
    gift wrapped
    on a Sunday morning.

CULT OF ONE

I've always been fascinated with cults.

Not necessarily the kind that hit the newspaper headlines, where maniacal bearded leaders deliver death to their grinning devotees. But more the everyday, almost *invisible cults*. The ones we find ourselves hopelessly drawn toward and frequently get trapped in.

Like the drunk buying a bottle of booze on a Monday morning.

The religious zealot who confuses faith with certainty, and attacks others for not sharing the same belief as them. Political junkies, who divide the world into left and right. Hurling insults at each other from the trenches, while the politicians line their pockets with thirty pieces of silver.

How we pin posters of pop idols and movie stars to our bedroom walls. Stalk *the followed* on social media. Wait patiently in the pouring rain, just to catch a glimpse of passing stardom. Screaming fans intoxicated by fame, addicted to celebrity— *monkeys watching other monkeys eat bananas.*

And then there's our endless pursuit for the next shiny trinket.

Fallen angels shopping for halos. Worshipping at the crumbling altar of commercialism. Emptying wallets and bankrupting our souls.

But perhaps it's the *Cult of Two* that interests me the most.

Where we chase butterflies disguised as romantic dreams—*the relentless desire to love, and be loved in return.*

Running from one relationship to the next. Hoping this time it will be different. Always forgetting that love is unpredictable, complicated, and wonderful in equal parts.

And when we come up empty-handed, we can't wait to push the self-destruct button.

Like how when a relationship ends, we often needlessly blame ourselves. Or waste even more of our precious energy pointing the finger at the other person. Rather than simply letting go and moving on—*the ultimate act of retribution.*

The truth is, *the harsh reality of love,* is that it's fickle, mostly fleeting, and seldom ticks every single box if we do find it.

Just as we have to come to terms with our own inherent flaws, we need to be open to accepting the limitations of others. This doesn't mean we have to sell ourselves short, or subscribe to second best. It's more about recognizing our individual differences and asking ourselves *can we honestly make this relationship work?*

Real love is not just the willingness to make it happen, but the absolute certainty that it can.

So please don't rush into love or put your life on hold waiting for it. Enjoy being blissfully single. Use this precious time to really get to know yourself. To discover who you are, what you really want—*and the future you so fucking deserve.*

While you're on this gorgeous inward adventure, go explore the wonderful world outside your bedroom window. Run away with the circus and never look back. Leave behind all the dumb expectations society expects of you, *the bullshit others put on you,* and create your own destiny.

Just be you.

In your amazing, dazzling, beautifully crazy—*Cult of One.*

—

Do you believe it's possible to find true love?

Yes—because I found you.

THANK YOU

Well, you finally made it to the end.

Hopefully you enjoyed our little roller-coaster ride together.

When you read the words again, and dive beneath the surface of the dark lake, you may find you're actually reading a very different book. *I did try to warn you the pages are bewitched.*

And if you're feeling particularly mischievous, go tell your friends about *Cult of Two.*

I also hope you get to read my other books, *Dirty Pretty Things, Bitter Sweet Love, Smoke & Mirrors,* and *Winter of Summers,* if you haven't already done so.

Please stay in touch on my official Facebook, Twitter, and Instagram pages. I always love to know which poems, pieces of prose, or short stories you liked the most.

Until we meet again, *in another time, another place,* may kindness be your guide.

Thank you so much for your wonderful support.

Best wishes always,

—Michael xo

ACKNOWLEDGMENTS

A warm thank you to my agent, Al Zuckerman. It was such a pleasure to catch up with you and Claire in New York. I certainly look forward to seeing you again soon for another wonderful evening of potent cocktails, stimulating conversation, gorgeous food, and exceptional wine.

Samantha Wekstein, thank you for all your help and support. I truly appreciate it. And thanks to the rest of the team at Writers House, New York.

A big thank you to Kirsty Melville, Patty Rice, and Kathy Hilliard for bringing my fifth book with Andrews McMeel into the world. I can't wait to buy you all a well-deserved martini!

Tinca Veerman, I simply can't thank you enough. I'm just so happy to have another one of your amazing artworks on the cover of *Cult of Two*.

To my son, Oliver, I love you more than all the mathematical equations and scientific formulae, whirling around inside your clever head. If only I was half as smart as you.

Mum, Dad, Genevieve, and Ryder, when you visited New Zealand this year, half of this book was already written. Given the number of fabulous lunches, fantastic dinners, glasses of whiskey, and bottles of wine, it's a miracle I recovered in time to write the rest. See you all again soon!

To Barry Houston, a grandfather to Oliver, and a wonderfully kind man to me, we will always miss you. Thank you for all the happy memories you gave to us.

Thank you to all my friends who never stop handing me a glass of wine and making me laugh.

And to all my lovely readers, thanks again for your support.

ABOUT THE AUTHOR

Michael Faudet is the author of the international bestsellers *Dirty Pretty Things*, *Bitter Sweet Love*, *Smoke & Mirrors*, and *Winter of Summers*. His books have been nominated in the Goodreads Choice Awards for Best Poetry. *Dirty Pretty Things* was also selected by Sylvia Whitman, the owner of the iconic Shakespeare and Company bookstore in Paris, as one of her personal favorite books of 2016.

He frequently explores the intricacies of love, loss, relationships, and sex in poetry, prose, and short stories. His lyrical and often sensual writing continues to attract readers from all around the world.

Before turning his hand to writing books, Michael enjoyed a successful career in advertising as an award-winning executive creative director. He managed creative departments and developed advertising campaigns for major brands in many countries.

Michael is represented by the literary agency Writers House, New York. He currently lives in New Zealand in a little house by the sea with girlfriend and author Lang Leav.

INDEX